Korean Children's Stories and Songs

Edited by Peter Hyun
Illustrated by Dong-il Park

HOLLYM

Elizabeth, NJ · SEOUL

Copyright © 1978, 1995
by Korean Overseas Information Service

First published in 1978
by Saem Toh Publishing Co.
1-115, Tongsung-dong, Chongno-gu, Seoul, Korea
Under the title of "It's Fun Being Young In Korea"

Revised edition, 1995
Second printing, 1998
by Hollym International Corp.
18 Donald Place, Elizabeth, New Jersey 07208, USA.
Tel: (908)353-1655   Fax: (908)353-0255
http:/www.hollym.com

Published simultaneously in Korea
by Hollym Corporation; Publishers
13-13 Kwanchol-dong, Chongno-gu, Seoul 110-111, Korea
Tel: (02)735-7554   Fax: (02)730-8192
http://www.hollym.co.kr

ISBN: 1-56591-065-6

Printed in Korea

Contents

Preface

This book is dedicated to the children of the world in commemoration of the International Year of the Child 1979.

Its purpose is to present a glimpse of the fantasies that occupied the minds and hearts of Korean children during the struggling years when the nation was known as the Hermit Kingdom, and, with the inclusion of three modern short stories, a brief picture of what the children of later generations were learning.

Although incomplete in that it does not contain every short story and poem of the land that has been preserved through the centuries, it is felt the ones gathered here are the most representative of this area of Korea's folklore and will offer the fairest cross-section.

It is hoped that through the publication and dissemination of books such as this the children of the world will learn that they are all very much alike.

Grateful acknowledgement is extended to:

Mrs. Lee Chung-wha Iyengar who translated Yoon Suk-joong's *Ten Fingers:*

M. A. Ball who translated *The Flower-Eating Locomotive* by Kim Yo-sup, and the songs *Half-Moon* by Yoon Kuk-Young, *Lullaby* by Park Mok-wol, *Flower Deer* by Yoo Kyung-hwan, *Eyes* by Kim Il-lo, and *My Little Puppy Dog* by Kim Sung-do;

Steven L. Shields who translated Lee Hyun-ju's *Dancing Village;* and the F. T. Yoon Co. which permitted *Little Spring, Come Pick the Moon, World Map,* and *Springtime Outing* to be reprinted from *Half Past Four: Poems for Children* (1978) by Yoon Suk-joong, translated by Francis Taewoon Yoon and D. D. Lapham.

Korean Children's Stories

The sign reads: From Tulip Station to Saturday Station

The Flower–Eating Locomotive

By Kim Yo-sup

If you spread out a map, you'll find a country whose border is made up of roses. The name of the country isn't important to the people who live there. If you ask the people about their national flag, they'll pick a flower blooming near them and give it to you, whether it is a jasmine or a tulip, a rose or a carnation, a lilac or a lily, a forget-me-not or a morning glory.

Now look above this map, and see the morning sunlight as it spreads across the sky. See the birds as they shake the dew from their wings and fly off like a bouncy rubber ball. Soon people begin to move about and all of the small countryside train stations bustle with activity. You can see a sign at every station:

From Jasmine Station to Adventure Station—39 km;
From Tulip Station to Saturday Station—52 km;
From . . .

In other countries the hands of clocks are pointing to twelve, one, or two o'clock, and in the country where the most common stations have flower names, a constant rat-a-tat-tat breaks the clear morning air near the stations. Now don't get the idea that it's the sound of shooting as in battle. No, it's the sound of a three-wheeled truck laden with produce as it rattles across the meadows, its wheels reflecting the golden rays of the sun. Not just of trucks, but also of pushcarts traveling toward the small stations with the flower name signs.

The engineer has already arrived at the station, and now he's sitting in a locomotive which is connected to a long line of freight cars. Instead of tooting the steam whistle for fun, he whistles to himself as he smokes his pipe.

Oh! Oh! A crisis! The train is preparing to depart! People race to the station, trying to push their carts to the front of the crowd. As the trucks and carts arrive people load flowers into the freight cars and then get in themselves. The flowers come from mountains, valleys, and fields all over the country. When the freight car is tightly packed with flowers the stationmaster wearing a hat with a gold braid, slowly waves a flower at the train. As soon as the engineer sees this signal he blows the whistle. With a sound like a pipe organ the blast soars up to Heaven. The smoke rising from the smokestack is shaped like flower petals, or the pipe between the engineer's teeth, or like a lion captured in Africa, or maybe it is the face of a philosopher whom the engineer respects.

With wheels spinning, the train starts out of the station with the flower name sign.

The train goes from one town to another. As the train crosses a trestle, thunder echoes back from the river. When high mountains rise up in front of the train, it makes a tunnel and goes through it. The train speeds along like a giant racing a hurricane.

Instead of smoke, the fragrance of jasmine and other flowers pours out of the smoke stack. If you think it's because this train is laden with flowers, you're right, but that's not the only reason. What the fireman burns is not coal. Bunches of flowers and the roots of flowering trees are burnt in the furnace. Once again the loud blast of the whistle spreads through the air. It is like the sound of a flock of skylarks crying. After a while, the train crosses over into the unguarded and

deseted border region, which is totally covered with rose petals. As the train enters the border zone its iron wheels spin ever faster and the fragrance of flowers gushes forth. The iron giant races through the neighboring countryside. Here in this common, ordinary countryside is a perfume factory. The country's sole export is flowers for making perfume. The people's sole occupation is growing the flowers from whence the petals come. The train's sole mission is carrying the petals to the perfume factory.

The country and its people are sending forth to the world outside the fragrance of love in the hopes that someday all will rush to catch the train that is pulled by the flower-eating locomotive.

The Dancing Village

By Lee Hyun-ju

If you have ever traveled to the southern part of Korea you have probably heard the story of the village of Choyong. People call this village "The Dancing Village." The reason for that is all the villagers like to dance.

Every year on the last day of December the people of this village make a huge bonfire on the banks of the lotus pond in the center of the village and have a dance festival.

Because these people dance so beautifully, it is not easy for others to imitate them. The villagers of Choyong like to watch dancing almost as well as they like to dance.

When the older people teach their young how to dance, they always start with a warning: "You will be able to dance only after you have learned how to watch others dance." So all of the village children start their training by learning how to watch others dance. When the children start thinking "I hope that the dancer's beads of sweat will roll from my forehead and that his breath will become my breath," they have already started to become wonderful dancers.

The people of this village were very careful with their dancing. They did not dance to live and eat, and they did not dance in order to celebrate. They did not dance to comfort the sad. Their dance was unlike any other dance in all of Korea.

The people of the dancing village had their dance festival every year so that they could bring back to memory the story of a young man who led a particularly sad life from the time he was born until the time he died in his early youth.

From the time he was just a child he had a talent that no one else had. That talent was dancing. His name was Choyong.

When Choyong danced he was as the wind. The branches of the nearby trees would quiver and the gathered clouds would depart. His dance gave comfort to the sad; it became a song to the happy, food for the hungry, and spring water for the thirsty.

The village people cherished Choyong as if he were a priceless jewel. No one in the village but Choyong could dance, but all the villagers loved to watch. The sad overcame their sadness; the happy sang their happiness; the thirsty were able to drink refreshing spring water. This is why they all treasured Choyong.

But Choyong never once danced for any particular reason. To him dancing was merely his life. Dancing was his sadness. Dancing was his happiness.

One year, on the last day of December, Choyong got the urge to go out into the big, wide world. He would ask himself, "How long must I live in this small village? I want to climb up the mountain and see what is on the other side. I want to go across the wide river. On the other side I will discover a world so much bigger than the world of this village. I might find many people waiting for me to show them my dance!"

When Choyong told the other villagers that he planned to leave the village, the oldest of all the villagers gave this warning to Choyong: "Young man, the world is big. But it can be a lot smaller than you think. There is nothing to stop you from leaving. If you want to leave, you may do so. But outside of the village, the world is small. Come back . . ." Then he added, but so Choyong could not hear, ". . . this village can be bigger than all the world."

Choyong respectfully thanked his elder for the advice, bowed and left the village. All of the sad-faced villagers gathered to bid him farewell.

The outside world, as if crazy, thronged Choyong. "He is the son of dance," they would say. Everyone would shout, "Hurrah for Choyong!" Wherever he went Choyong received a big welcome. People would shout and clap their hands.

One day a short, fat man took Choyong aside and wispered in his ear, "Let me borrow your dance. I am a charity worker and have organized a ten-hour long charity festival to raise some money for flood victims. If you will join us, the festival will be a success."

Choyong was a bit uneasy. He asked, "You say 'charity'? Very well, but I do

not know how I can lend you my dance."

The charity worker slapped his fat belly and laughed, "You leave that to me," he said. "All you need do is dance your dance on my stage."

Finally Choyong was standing on the stage. He began to dance for the number-less spectators who had come and paid money to watch.

After the dance had ended and all of the spectators had gone home, the charity worker put his arms around the mountain of money piled in the empty theater and cried out, "What a wonderful success." Tears of happiness streamed down his face. In the meantime, Choyong was trying to calm his troubled heart. He feared that the charity worker was not really a charity worker. He felt bad that he had danced for all of those money-paying spectators. He felt as if he had lost all that he had. Little by little he began to be more troubled, and as with an illness that cannot be cured, Choyong realized that it was too late. He had already danced. He could not change what had happened in the past. At those thoughts he became even sadder.

Even during the time that Choyong was feeling sorry for himself, the charity worker's stomach became even larger. Everytime they moved to a new town, the charity worker would change his name. Many months passed.

One day the charity worker came to Choyong with a very serious face and said, "Choyong, this time our work is very important. You will dance before the King. It is the King's birthday. Lately, for some reason, the King has been very unhappy. This is the best opportunity we have ever had. If you can make the King happy, he might give you a high government office." Upon hearing these words, Choyong laughed inside himself.

For the first time, since leaving his home, Choyong dreamed of his village. In his dream familiar people warmly greeted his tired self.

"I see," said Choyong. "It is a good opportunity, indeed." Choyong gave the charity worker a big hug. The charity worker muttered to himself, "It really is a good opportunity, is it not? Who knows, it may be our last."

Finally, Choyong was standing on the special stage that had been prepared for the King's birthday. At the foot of the stage, countless people were waiting, with the King himself, to see Choyong's dance.

Slowly lifting his feet and waving his arms, he began to dance. His face was cover-ed with sweat and his heart was trembling deep inside his chest. Slowly the dance got faster and as it ripened to a climax the people watched, hardly daring to breathe.

"For the King!"

Crying, Choyong said, "No! No!" Then, in a moment, the small whirling body of Choyong fell from the high stage as a leaf falls from the tree. The people were shocked. By the time they got to him, Choyong was covered with blood as was the ground around him.

The King was furious. "Get rid of him as he is—at once!" he shouted. On the King's order, a few men took Choyong's limp body and threw it in a nearby gully.

Now since Choyong had left his village, every year on the last day of December, the village folk would gather at the banks of the lotus pond in the center of town and by the light of a bonfire, would share stories about the dance of Choyong.

One year, just two days before the last day of December, an unfamiliar beggar came into town. The villagers knew most of the beggars who wandered into town, and generally they treated them with disregard, but this particular one was new to everyone. He had never been seen before. He was a hunchback and this made him stand out. His face was ugly and scarred.

The hunchback beggar accepted the cold rice that the village people grudgingly gave him. He would disappear in the evening but every morning he would re-appear. No one was able to find out where he spent the night.

The last day of the year arrived and the village people gathered at the lotus

pond. The burning bonfire helped the people once again to remember the story of the dance of Choyong. As they were gathered, a dark shadow started coming closer to the crowd, but no one noticed.

Someone broke the silence and asked. "Do you think Choyong is still dancing?" No one answered. Then someone else asked: "Do you think Choyong still remembers our village?" Again no one answered. By this time the dark shadow had made its way to the edge of the crowd. One older man started crying and asked, "Choyong, won't you please dance for us now?" Just as the old man was finishing his question, the black shadow darted into the midst of the crowd. In the light of the fire, they all saw the hunchback beggar who had come two days previously. The hunchback's ugly back began to twist and he started to dance a very strange dance. Little by little the movements of his arms and legs began to get faster. By the light of the bonfire tears could be seen streaming down his face.

After a while someone cried out, "It's Choyong! It's Choyong's dance!" The voice was choked with tears.

The hunchback seemed not to know how to stop. It looked as if he was stuck to the ground and then like a butterfly he soared up into the sky. He was spinning so fast that his feet could not be seen. Suddenly, he stopped and stood looking up into Heaven—his shoulders moving as he breathed. The village people stood wordless, tears filling their eyes.

Then, the hunchback suddenly fell to the ground. The villagers took a lantern and went to him, but they were too late. He had already stopped breathing. Choyong's face looked as if he were peacefully sleeping.

From then on everyone called the village, "The Village of Choyong."

Even today, if you go there on the last day of December, the people of the village of Choyong will be having their dance festival. But there is one thing that you must clearly understand. Their dance is not for you to enjoy—it is for the people of the village of Choyong to always remember the sad life and tragic death of the young man, Choyong.

Ten Fingers

By Yoon Suk-joong

1. The Woolen Mittens Knit by Mother

"Mom, I don't want to eat supper," said Youngi. He had eaten only a couple of spoonfuls of rice when he said this, then crawled under his blanket which was lying on the warmest part of the heated floor. He began to cough.

"Are you sick?" his mother asked as she rushed to Youngi and touched his forehead. He was hot with fever.

"No, Mother. I'm fine," he said as he continued to cough.

"You must have caught a cold while you were out there sledding. I told you to quit playing and come inside but you didn't."

Hiding his head underneath the blanket, Youngi turned red trying to hold back his coughs. His right hand, which was covering his mouth, began to shiver.

The fingers had committed a crime earlier. In the afternoon, when Youngi was sitting at his desk, he was leafing quickly through the pages of a picture book without looking at the pictures. He wetted his right thumb and then, with the aid of his index finger, turned the pages. After a while, the five fingers of his left hand snatched the book away and threw it on the floor.

"How boring!"

Youngi went outside and rode his sled all day with neighborhood children. The five fingers of his left hand made Youngi go outside. The ten fingers without mittens shivered in the cold, and yet the fun of riding the sled made them forget about the chill.

His mother placed a pillow under his head and covered him with a blanket. Youngi's fingers slid inside the blanket and whispered.

"Youngi got cold because of us. Had we held on to the picture book, Youngi would have spent the day in a warm room. He would never have gotten cold. Also, it was we who made Youngi slide fast on a sled with cold hands."

Youngi's mother thought otherwise. "Had I finished the woolen mittens, Youngi would have worn them and his hands would have been warm. It was my fault."

Mother took out the half-finished mittens and a roll of woolen yarn that had been pierced with knitting needles. The little finger peeped through the blanket and noticed Youngi's mother knitting. When the little finger told the other fingers, all the fingers were glad. They would have clapped together had Youngi not been sleeping so soundly.

"She must be almost finished knitting by now," the fingers thought after a while. The thumb crawled out of the blanket and looked outside. "Heavens! What shall we do?" the thumb said to the other fingers. "Mother has fallen asleep."

Mother was indeed tired. She had been working since dawn outside, and the warmth of the room made her fall asleep, holding the knitting needles in her hands.

Youngi's fingers tried to wake mother up. Instead of shaking mother's hand, the fingers touched the sharp end of a needle and Youngi screamed: "Ouch!" Mother woke up at the sound.

"My goodness, you are such a wild sleeper," said his mother.

Sometime after midnight, the mittens were completed. Mother placed the finished mittens under Youngi's mattress and went to bed. The snow fell softly outside.

2. The Thumb That Was Hit by a Hammer

When the weather became very cold, Youngi's father bought a cap with a round woolen bell on the top—just the kind Youngi had seen in a dream. In his dream, the bell on the top of the cap did not ring. The bell attached to the newly-bought cap did not ring either.

"This bell does not ring."

"But it can wiggle and dance instead. Why don't you try it on" said his mother placing the cap over Youngi's head.

"It fits you just right."

"Do you think this will fit me next year and the year after that?"

"Of course. The cap was knit with woolen yarn. It will expand with your head so that it will fit you year after year after year."

Youngi smiled a wide smile. He took very good care of the cap bought by his father and the mittens knit by his mother. When he went outside, he didn't wear his mittens. Instead he hung the string to which the mittens were attached over his shoulder. At home he read and ate with his cap on for fear that someone might step on it.

Each night before he went to bed, he climbed on a box to reach a nail on which to hang his woolen mittens and cap.

For a few days he performed this duty faithfully. But he slowly got tired of the routine of having to bring a box to reach the nail. He started to hang the mittens by throwing them by the string as he would a jump rope. He threw the cap over the nail as if he were throwing a ball into a basket. Later he became tired of even doing this, and he would scatter his mittens and cap on the floor after school. Mother had to pick them up and hang them on the nail.

"Our Youngi is developing a bad habit," said his mother disapprovingly. Sometimes she glared at him.

Then Youngi thought: "I don't have a bad habit. It is the nail that is placed too high for me.

Youngi was right. No matter where he went, the nails were placed too high so that children had a hard time reaching them. Grown-ups can hang up clothes easily. But poor children have to stand on tiptoe or bring a box to stand on. It was not fair for a child to put up with such inconveniences day after day. No wonder children got cranky too.

"I've got an idea." Youngi rushed to the front porch and got a carpenter's box which his father had put away. He came into the room and took out a hammer and nail. He looked for a place to drive the nail in. It had to be at just the right height.

"How clever I am." Mumbling to himself, Youngi found a spot where he could put the nail.

"I am going to hit now." He raised his right hand, closed his eyes, and brought the hammer down hard.

"Ouch!"

Youngi let go of the hammer, covered his left thumb with his right hand, and jumped around in pain. Instead of hitting the nail, the hammer had landed on Youngi's left thumb.

"What's the matter?" Mother, who was working in the kitchen, rushed to the room.

The left thumb turned blue and the rest of the fingers of Youngi's left hand seemed pale and shivering. The five fingers of Youngi's right hand dropped down feeling embarassed and sorry. Mother held Youngi's fingers in her hands tightly and said, "That's all right. You are going to be all right."

3. Washing the Face With One Hand

Mother bandaged the swollen red and blue thumb. As she did this, Youngi felt a hot pulsating pain.

"What if my thumb is seriously injured?" he cried.

"Don't worry, Youngi," said mother. "Although it is very painful, your thumb did not bleed. I think by tomorrow the swelling will go down." Saying this, she shoved the hammer, which was lying on the floor, under the desk. As she pushed it, it met the nail which had rolled under the desk in order to avoid the attack of the hammer.

"Dear nail, how did you manage to avoid being hit?" the hammer asked.

"Please, hammer, don't talk about it. I am sure that one day I will have to be hit on the head. How can I relax when I know what fate awaits me?"

"Your fate is unavoidable. Nails are born to be beaten. Hammers and mallets are born to hit other things. Knowing that I might some day hit you makes me ashamed to face you."

The nail and hammer decided that, although it was unfortunate that Youngi had hit his thumb with the hammer, they were not altogether sorry he had hurt himself. Maybe it would make him realize what nails and hammers had to bear.

"Youngi must appreciate us now," they thought.

Whether or not Youngi realized what the hammer and nail had to put up with, he did find out how helpless his fingers were without his thumb.

The next morning, Youngi had a hard time washing his face. Trying not to wet his heavily bandaged left thumb, he put his left hand on his knee and bent over the washbasin. He got his clothes wet instead of his face. Mother quickly wrapped a towel around Youngi's neck and rubbed a bit of soap on his face before she rinsed it clean.

"My goodness. Look at the dirt around your neck," she said. "A black crow would mistake you for his uncle." Rubbing the dirt from Youngi's neck she laughed. "Our Youngi has become a baby again. He has to have his face washed by his mother."

Padugi, the family puppy, wagged its tail as if amused by the sight of Youngi having his face washed. This annoyed Youngi, who tried to throw water at the dog.

Mother held his arm and said, "You are like a man who is slapped at the East Gate of the city and blames a man at the West Gate. Why do you scold Padugi because you have to have someone wash your face? Padugi is an easy target to blame for your problems."

Youngi had as much trouble eating breakfast as he had trying to wash his face. He tried to scoop up rice from a bowl with a spoon, but the rice was hard to scoop because he couldn't steady the bowl with his other hand.

Getting dressed was a big problem for Youngi. When he tried to put on his trousers, his right leg kept getting caught in the left side, and he almost fell. The buttons on his jacket didn't obey his one hand either. The books were difficult to put into their bag because the lid of the bag kept flipping shut, since Youngi couldn't hold it open with his hurt hand and the normal hand was trying to hold the books.

Because of one injured thumb, all routine tasks became difficult for Youngi. Washing his face, eating breakfast and getting dressed were very hard. It seemed impossible for him to tie his shoes because the strings kept getting looser rather than tighter.

"Even the shoestrings are making fun of me!" Youngi cried as he took them off and threw them across the room.

"Youngi, the shoes haven't done anything wrong. It is because your thumb is hurt that you cannot tie them," said mother as she retrieved the shoes. She put them on Youngi's feet and tied them. Then she took his hand and walked part of the way to school with him. Youngi's woolen mittens hung sadly on their nail, waiting for him to return.

4. To Hit the Right Thumb With the Right Hand

As Youngi walked toward the front gate of the school, one of his shoelaces came untied, and he kept stepping on it. He went to a nearby shop and peeked inside. An old shopkeeper, who was looking outside through a small hole in the glass, stopped puffing on his pipe, shook ashes from it and opened the shop's sliding door.

"What can I do for you?" he asked Youngi.

Youngi hesitated. "Sir, I didn't come here to buy anything. I was hoping that you would tie my shoe for me."

"What? Have your hands run away from you?"

"No, Sir. My hands are still here, but I cannot use one, because I hurt my thumb. It is hard to tie shoelaces with only one hand."

"Now I've heard of everything," said the shopkeeper. "How can you stick your foot out in front of an adult and ask him to tie your shoe?" He began to turn red with anger. Youngi did not know that the man was not angry at the request but rather because his business was so poor.

"Will you tie it for me if I buy something from you, Sir?"

"That would be wrong because it would mean you are paying for my service,"

the shopkeeper replied. "No, I cannot do that." As he spoke those words, the shopkeeper tied the shoe.

Youngi bowed many times in gratitude. As he rushed toward school, he yelled, "I will buy drawing paper and a notebook on my way home, Sir."

The shopkeeper was happy to hear the promise, and he even bowed his head a little. "Thanks very much."

In spite of the pain, the bandaged thumb felt happy that Youngi would be buying something from the old shopkeeper.

As soon as Youngi went into the class his classmates surrounded him and began asking him questions.

"How did it happen?"

"Did you slam a door on it?"

"Did you cut it with a knife?"

"Did a thorn prick you?"

"Were you bitten by a dog?"

"Were you burnt by fire?"

"Did you stick your thumb into ice?"

Nobody could guess how Youngi had gotten hurt. All the children clustered

around Youngi and listened as he told his story. They realized there was hardly any child who had not hurt a finger sometime in his life. The boy who asked whether Youngi had slammed a door on his finger, had almost crushed his finger in a door a few years ago. The boy who had asked whether Youngi cut his finger with a knife, had once got a splinter under his nail while making a kite with bamboo sticks. The boy who had asked whether Youngi was bitten by a dog, had once tried to snatch a ball from the mouth of a dog. The dog had accidentally sunk his teeth into the boy's thumb. The boy who had asked whether Youngi had burned himself, had burned both his right thumb and little finger while roasting chestnuts. The boy who asked whether Youngi's finger had been stuck in ice, once made a snowman without wearing gloves. His fingers became red and swollen afterward.

One child, who had kept quiet while the boys chattered away about Youngi's finger, stuck out his thumb which had a crushed nail.

"Look at my right thumb!" he cried. "I was making a sled out of a wooden apple crate. I hit my thumb with a hammer, and this is what happened!"

A boy spoke out in the midst of the noise. "That's a lie. How can you hit your right thumb holding a hammer in your right hand?"

But it was not a lie. The boy was left-handed.

5. A Picture Drawn by a Finger

It was time for athletics. Each boy took his cap from his book bag and ran outside, screaming loudly. When Youngi started toward the playground with the rest of the children, the homeroom teacher stopped him.

"Youngi, you'd better stay in the classroom since you have a sore thumb. Stay near the stove and read a book if you like. Be careful with the hammer next time. Your accident could have been a disaster." Saying this, the teacher patted Youngi's head.

The right hand that had blundered with the hammer quietly crawled into the pocket feeling embarassed. The bruised thumb also dragged the rest of his four fingers into another pocket as if he, too, was ashamed. The teacher smiled and said, "What did I tell you? I told you not to put your fingers into your pockets. What if you trip over something with your hands in your pockets? That's not all. You should not stand in front of a teacher with your hands in your pockets no matter how cold they may be."

"We didn't come inside the pockets just because we were cold, did we?" one hand asked the other.

"Of course not. We were afraid of being scolded. That's why we came in."

"Why don't you tell the teacher not to talk about something he doesn't understand?"

While Youngi's fingers were talking among themselves, the teacher turned around and went outside. In the empty classroom, Youngi warmed himself near the stove for a while, then he looked toward the window. He could not see outside. He went near the window wondering why he could not see outside. The window was coated with a thin sheet of ice. During the clear, windless night before, frost had spread over the ground, grass, chimneys and window panes. The morning was cold because of the wind and the frost had not yet disappeared.

The square, frosted window panes looked just like paper. Youngi started to draw a picture with his right index finger. It was a drawing of the fingers next to his hurt thumb. Youngi got excited and kept drawing hands with five spread fingers. He wanted to draw as many hands as the students in the class had. There were fifty-one students in the class, so he would have to draw one hundred and two hands. One hundred and two hands mean five hundred and ten fingers. It would be hard to draw so many fingers in the time he had, but Youngi kept on drawing, filling in the lower part of the window.

He brought a desk and climbed on it so that he could reach the upper parts of the window. The index finger, whose job was to indicate something to others, did not realize until now how much fun it was to draw. When the finger itself did not do a good job, the hardened nail came to its rescue with a screeching sound. The window now was full of the drawings of fingers. At a quick glance the fingers looked like clusters of maple leaves. The leaves looked as if they were alive and dancing in a breeze.

The bell rang ending the gym period.

"Oh, my goodness! What shall I do?" Youngi's heart pounded. He did not want the teacher to find the drawings because the children were not allowed to draw on the windows.

He had to erase the drawings so he would not get caught. But how could he erase so many fingers in a short time? The bell, which Youngi had always looked forward to, now became a menacing threat, like the warning of a fire engine.

The children were already entering the classroom. Youngi slumped down in his chair and placed his head on his desk.

6. An Event That Occurred on a Warm Winter Day

"Wow! What are those?" the children asked as they gathered around the window.
"Heavens, I see nothing but fingers," one child said.
"I wonder who did this?"
"It's obvious. Only the one who stayed alone in the classroom could have done it."
"Wait till the teacher comes in."
The children talked loudly as they glanced occasionally at Youngi.

"What is this? This is not a stretched hand, but a fist."

"It must be the fist of the Alley General."

In Youngi's class, there was a boy nicknamed Alley General. He was a bully, who acted like a mouse in front of a stronger boy, but bullied weaker ones by hitting them with his fist.

The Alley General, upon hearing this, glared at Youngi and threatened, "You,

you! You want me to beat you up?"

Ook, who was Youngi's friend in class, blocked the way and said, "Look more carefully. That fist is too big for you. I think that fist belongs to Teacher Kang of the the third grade. You know how he goes around showing off his fist, ready to hit someone. Youngi must have thought of him and drawn the big fist. Isn't that right, Youngi?"

At this moment, the homeroom teacher opened the classroom door and came in. He looked around the room before ordering the students to return to their seats. The teacher walked deliberately toward his desk and then looked at the drawings on the window for a while.

"I heard it was done by Youngi," someone whispered to him.

Youngi's heart began to pound.

"Youngi, you will be surely scolded," a child said.

As the children began to make noise, the teacher raised his voice.

"This is too much noise. Everyone quiet! It is time to study. Take out your books. Don't look sideways."

But one child kept glancing at the window.

"Chang Mu Swe, what did I tell you?" the teacher said. "Didn't I tell you to keep your eyes on your work?" The teacher hit his desk hard with his palm.

The frightened children looked straight ahead holding on to their textbooks. They held their breaths waiting for the teacher to speak. He usually was fond of telling funny stories, but was in a stern mood today. Youngi thought that the teacher was angry because of the drawings on the window.

When the class was almost over, the teacher said slowly. "Why were you making such a commotion earlier?"

There was no response.

"That's okay. You may speak out."

Again no one spoke.

"Then I am going to ask you a question. What is the definition of scribbling on the wall?"

One student raised his hand.

"It means writing or drawing anything on places like a wall, pillar or window."

"That's right. Tell me why you were all teasing Youngi and making noise?"

"It was because Youngi drew fingers and a big fist on the window."

The teacher smiled for the first time. "Where are the drawings of fingers? Are they invisible to a teacher's eyes." The children all looked toward the window. The teacher was right. There were no traces of drawings.

"That's strange. I wonder what happened?"

The sun had come out and melted the frost. Youngi's drawings had melted also.

7. An Ill-Tempered Wind

It was recess time. All the children went out to play, except Youngi who had hurt his thumb. Since it was too hot near the stove, Youngi gathered his books and drawing papers and went near the window. The sunshine which had melted his drawings on the window was brighter and warmer than before, and erased even the water droplets which had formed from the melted frost. The window looked even clearer than one just polished by human hands. It was so clear a sparrow dashed toward the window and almost hit the glass. The sunshine warmed Youngi and his back was wet with sweat.

"Gee, it's hot! Maybe I will open the window a little."

He opened the window wide. As if the wind had waited for this moment, it came rushing in and blew a piece of drawing paper onto the teacher's desk. Youngi stood up quickly and ran after the paper. As he tried to pick it up, the clumsy, bandaged thumb hit a bottle of red ink. The loose lid of the bottle came off and red ink splashed all over the drawing paper. He closed the bottle quickly, but the ink had already spilled all over the teacher's desk.

Youngi tried to wipe it off with a piece of cloth but the red color did not come off. The drawing paper on which the red ink was spilled could be hidden inside a desk, but the red spots on the teacher's desk could not be hidden. The left thumb, which had blundered, began to shake. The other four fingers of the left hand and the five fingers of the right hand all trembled in fear that the teacher would scold Youngi. Even his arms shivered in fear at the thought of being punished. His legs began to shake.

"What shall I do?"

Youngi stamped on the floor in dismay as the bell rang. The students and the teacher came inside.

Youngi, who could not run away or hide, began to cry loudly. The hurt thumb, which felt sorry for Youngi, lifted itself toward his eyes to wipe off the tears with the bandage.

"It was my fault. I am sorry. Don't cry." The thumb tried to console him, but Youngi started to cry even harder.

The teacher, who had thought Youngi's thumb was bleeding, rushed to Youngi to hug him. Then he noticed that Youngi was not hurt, that the red liquid was just ink, and he sighed with relief.

The teacher asked Youngi how he had spilled the ink. Youngi told him the whole story.

The children who had teased Youngi over the drawings on the window now felt sorry for him. They sat quietly. The teacher laughed loudly after listening to the story. "Oh, it wasn't your fault, Youngi."

"Then whose fault was it?"

The students waited for the teacher's answer.

"It was that ill-tempered wind that spilled the ink," the teacher said. "Instead of running after the paper, Youngi should have closed the window. That's what you should have done. Do you understand, Youngi?"

"Yes, Sir." Youngi smiled, lifting his tear-stained face.

8. Cold Winter Depicted in a Drawing

It was time for art.

"What shall we draw today? How about a portrayal of a cold winter?" the teacher said.

Everyone took out drawing paper and crayons and began to draw. Some children propped their chins on their arms trying to think of good ideas.

Youngi drew in earnest, hiding his picture with one hand so that no one could see it.

The teacher, curious to see what the children were drawing, went around the classroom holding his hands behind his back. One child had drawn footprints that walked toward the middle of the paper, then turned around and went back.

"This picture is incomplete, isn't it?"

"No, Sir. It's complete, Sir."

"You have nothing but footsteps which turn around in the middle."

"Yes, Sir. You are right. I left the paper white because the scene was completely covered with snow. The direction of the footprints indicates that a man walked outside in the cold. He couldn't go any further because of the cold. That's why he turned around and went home, Sir."

"I see. That really shows a cold winter day. It certainly make sense."

The next picture was a snowman, with legs, walking toward a kitchen.

"Why does it want to go to the kitchen?"

"It is so cold, the snowman wants to warm himself near the fire."

"Oh! This picture makes good sense too."

The next picture was a grandfather who had a beard of icicles. It was so cold the old man's whiskers had frozen.

Another drawing was of a country house with a thatched roof. A row of many shoes was on the stone step leading into the room.

"What's this? I told you to depict a cold winter. You drew nothing but shoes."

The teacher flipped to the other side of the drawing and read out the student's name. "Kum Pawi, you must explain what this is about."

"Yes, Sir. That too is a cold winter day. It was too cold for anyone to go outside. The shoes on the stepping stone indicate that all the people are inside the room."

The children and the teacher laughed.

"This picture also makes sense after listening to the explanation," the teacher said.

After looking through the pile of pictures one by one, the teacher picked up the very last picture, which had been drawn by Youngi. Youngi, who had handed in the work shyly, with the picture side down, had returned to his chair with his head bowed.

When the teacher saw the picture, his eyes opened wide. The drawing was done on the piece of paper which had flown away when Youngi opened the window. Youngi took advantage of the ink-smeared paper. He had used the red smears effectively to show the hot dazzling sun. But the mountains below were still covered

with snow. Even the heat of the sun could not melt the snow on the mountains. So one could guess how cold it must have been.

The teacher lifted the picture high and showed it to the children who were anxious to know the name of the artist. "Today's first prize for depicting a cold winter day goes to Youngi. Here he showed the snow covered mountains, which defy the heat of the sun."

9. The Voice of Freedom in Darkness

After school Youngi rolled up the prize drawing, and proudly left through the school gate. He passed the little shop where he paused and mumbled to himself, "Oh, yes. I promised the shopkeeper I would buy drawing paper and a notebook."

He turned around and went inside the little shop. After buying the paper and a notebook, he spread out his picture and then put his right thumb up.

"Sir, do you know what my teacher said about this? He said he would present this to the International Children's Art Exhibition next spring."

"Really? You must be excited. Better take it home right away and show it to your mother."

Youngi hummed as he walked homeward. The neighborhood women were chatting in an alley and watched the smiling Youngi come home.

"Something good must have happened to our Youngi," they said.

"Did you win a prize or something?" one lady asked.

Youngi lifted his drawing and then put his right thumb up.

"I was right. You got first prize in a drawing contest, right?"

As soon as Youngi reached home, he knocked at the gate and called out for his mother. She came out from the kitchen, wiping her hands on her apron, and opened the gate.

"Mom! Mom! My drawing got a prize." Youngi stuck out his thumb once more. "Take a look at my picture."

He spread out the paper in front of his mother. Mother stepped back a little and said, "You certainly draw well."

That night Youngi went to bed early, because he was very tired. After he was asleep, his mother quietly picked up the drawing and pasted it on the wall.

That night Youngi's work was talked about at school, at the shop and at home. But the poor thumb on the left hand was restless and could not fall asleep. It was

suffocating inside the dark bandage. The thumb had not seen daylight for a day and half. It was bad enough being bandaged, but whenever it crawled out of the blanket, mother would cover it up right away. The thumb kept wiggling under the blanket.

"Youngi is not sleeping soundly because of the light," said his mother as she turned the light off.

The hurt thumb felt terrible. Things could not have been worse—bandaged, blanketed and now the light turned off.

"I've got an idea." The left thumb crawled out of the blanket, reached for the desk, and began to rub the bandage against a corner of the desk.

"Sh . . . ." Mother, who thought it was a rat making the noise, hit the desk. Youngi's thumb paused, but started rubbing again.

Finally the bandage slipped off. "Success! I've made it."

The liberated thumb lifted itself high. The right hand also crawled out of the blanket and lifted itself up.

"Hurrah!" Youngi's ten fingers cried out in the dark.

10. Five Pairs of Twins, Ten Fingers

Youngi, who awoke in the night, fumbled with his fingers. He could not find his painting.

"What happened to my picture?"

At his loud shout, his mother woke up and said in a sleepy voice: "Do you want your picture? I have hung it on the wall so that it won't get wrinkled. It is a long way from dawn. You better sleep some more."

His mother must have fallen asleep again. Youngi touched his left thumb in the darkness. It hurt when he pressed it. But he could bend and stretch it without feeling pain. He closed his eyes once more and went over what happened at school.

"The reason why the picture turned out well was because my hurt thumb tipped over the ink bottle. Then I will have to thank my left thumb." Youngi shook his head. "That's not right. The wind blew the drawing paper toward the ink bottle. I will have to thank the wind." He shook his head again. "That's not right. I opened the window because the sun was too hot. Because of the sun my picture turned out to be good." He shook his head once more. "That's not right. The cloud which had covered the sun lifted, and let the sunshine in. I must thank the cloud." Youngi thought some more. "The wind chased the clouds away. So I am back to thanking the wind."

Youngi blinked his eyes in the darkness trying hard to thank the right object but without success. "Who is it that made all these things happen?" Youngi thought for a long time.

"Now I know! It must be God, our Creator." Youngi clapped his hands.

The window brightened. It was morning. Mother was awakened by the clapping sound.

"Were you dreaming, Youngi?" his mother asked.

"No, Mother, I was awake. By the way, where is Dad?"

"Your Dad had to stay at the company again last night."

Youngi's father was a bus driver. At the crack of dawn, he went off to work, and returned only after Youngi had fallen asleep at night. Lately, Youngi hardly saw his father because he frequently had to work throughout the night.

"At this rate I might forget the face of my father," he complained.

"You are right. And your father may forget your face," his mother said.

Youngi thought of his father because he wanted to show off his drawing. Daddy would be so pleased to see his work. He might even paste the picture on the windshield of his bus, Youngi thought. "That would be a disaster. We must not ruin the picture. I can show it to him after it wins a prize at the International Children's Art Exhibition."

It became much brighter outside the window. Mother was already making clattering noises in the kitchen, preparing breakfast. Youngi, while he was still in bed, spread his arms toward the window. Lovely rays of light streamed through his spread fingers and tickled his face.

He looked carefully at the left thumb under the sunlight. The swelling had

subsided. He could move the thumb freely although parts around the nail remained blue.

It was quiet in the kitchen. Mother must have gone out to fetch some water.

Youngi, still in his pajamas, knelt on the mattress. He held his hands together in imitation of a girl in prayer, as in a picture which his father had pasted in a corner of the bus windshield.

"Dear God, please make my wish come true. I hope my drawing will win a prize in the International Children's Art Exhibition."

Youngi looked at his hands which were held together. Two thumbs were together. So were the two index fingers, middle fingers, fourth fingers and the little fingers. They were five pairs of twins which resembled each other.

He held tight the five pairs of twins and prayed again. "Please, God, make spring come soon."

Korean Children's
Songs

Springtime Outing

By Yoon Suk-joong

Lily, lily, golden bell
Pluck it, put it in your bill.
Bunch of chickies, hop, hop, hop.
Springtime outing, off they go.

POM NA TU RI
(SPRINGTIME OUTING)

Music: Kwon Tae-ho

NA RI NA RI KAE NA RI   IP BEH TTA TA MUL KO YO

PYONG AH   RI TTEH CHONG CHONG CHONG POM NA TU RI   KAM NI TA

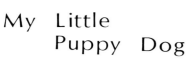

My Little
Puppy Dog

By Kim Sung-do

Waking from a sound sleep,
All alone, you cry.
You're mama's little baby,
My little puppy dog.

Digging underneath my skirts,
Safe from any harm,
You're mama's little baby,
My little puppy dog.

When you laugh upon my breast
And sweetly smile at me,
You're mama's little baby,
My little puppy dog.

Lullaby

By Park Mok-wol

Gee-ahm, gee-ahm,
In spite of winds,
In spite of drcams,
Our body falls asleep.

Ja-jang, ja-jang,
White butterfly bites

A sweet sound sleep
And brings it to our baby.

O-rum, o-rum,
Drowsiness comes
To eyebrows and ears
Of our soundly sleeping baby.

Ja-jang, ja-jang,
The spirit
Of the silver star
Has sent a sweet, sound sleep.

ONG TAL SAM
(LITTLE SPRING)

KIP UN SAN—SOK ONG TAL SAM NU KA WA SO MOK NA YO

SAE PYO KEH TO KKI KA NUN PI PI KO IH RO NA

SEH SU HA RO WAT TA KA MUL MAN MOK KO KA CHI YO

Little Spring

By *Yoon Suk-joong*

Deep in the mountain a little spring,
Who comes for a drink from this spring?

The rabbits at the break of day,
Rubbing their eyes when they awake,
Come to the spring to wash their faces,
They drink only, then go away.

Clear and clean water the little spring,
Who comes for a drink from this little spring?

In the moonlit night the roe deer,
Hide-and-seek, the game they play.
They become thirsty, rush to here;
After a quick drink, they go away.

53

Come Pick the Moon

By Yoon Suk-joong

Come on, boys, come on out!
Let's go get the moon.
Bring a bamboo stick and a gunnysack
To the hills out back.

Go on to the hills out back,
Climb high up back and back.

Pick the moon with the bamboo stick,
Put it in a gunnysack.

Over at Soonhee's house,
They can't afford to light the lamp.
When night comes, I hear,
Mending they cannot do.

Come on, boys, come on out!
Let's pluck the moon,
And hang it up there
In Soonhee's mommy's room.

TAL TTA RO KA CHA
(COME PICK THE MOON)

Music : Park Tae-hyun

AE TUL A NA O NO RA TAL TTA RO KA CHA

CHANG TAE TUL KO MANG TAE MAE KO TWIT TONG SAN U RO

TWIT TONG SAN EH OL RA KA MU TUNG' UL TA KO

CHANG— TAE RO TAL UL TA SO MANG TAE EH TAM CHA

Half-Moon

Yoon Kuk-young

In a small, white boat
In the blue sky
Are a cinnamon tree and a rabbit.
Without sail and without oar,
Yet gliding,
Gliding smoothly to a western shore.

Sailing across the Milky Way
To the land of clouds.
Where does it journey
Beyond the land of clouds?
Towards the sparkling reflection
So far away,
To the beacon light of a new dawn.
Now, child, find a road.

PAN TAL
(HALF—MOON)

PU RUN HA NUL UN—HA SU   HA YAN CHOK PAE EN —

KYE SU NA MU HAN —NA MU   TO KKI HAN MA   RI —

mp
TOT TAE TO   A   NI TAL KO   SAT TAE TO OP   SI —

f
KA   KI   TO CHAL TO KAN TA   SO—CHOK NA   RA   RO

Eyes

By Kim Il-lo

Baby's mother gone away
A tear forms, a jewel.

Baby's mother here to stay
A smile forms, a flower.

Twinkle of the morning star,
Our baby's eyes.

World Map

By Yoon Suk-joong

My homework is to draw a map of the world.
I drew and drew all last night, but
I haven't finished half of it yet.

Without your country or my country,
Without your nation or my nation,
If the world were just one big country,
How easy to make, my world map would be.

Flower Deer

By Yoo Kyung-hwan

Baby has a new quilt,
Quilt of flower deer.

Soft and fluffy cotton
Quilt of flower deer.

Sweetly sleeping baby
Faraway in dreamland.

Ride the flower deer away;
Ride the flower deer and play.